1 9 8 1
The Year
I Was Born

Compiled by Sally Tagholm

Illustrated by Michael Evans

FANTAIL

in association with Signpost Books

FANTAIL PUBLISHING, AN IMPRINT OF PUFFIN ENTERPRISES
Published by the Penguin Group
27 Wrights Lane London W8 5TZ, England
Viking Penguin Inc., 40 West 23rd Street, New York, NY 10010, USA
Penguin Books Australia, Ltd., Ringwood, Victoria, Australia
Penguin Books Canada, Ltd., 2801 John Street, Markham, Ontario,
Canada L3R 1B4
Penguin Books Ltd., Registered Offices: Harmondsworth, Middlesex,
England
Published by Penguin Books in association with Signpost Books

First published 1990
10 9 8 7 6 5 4 3 2

Based on an original idea by Sally Wood
Conceived, designed and produced by Signpost Books Ltd, 1989
Copyright in this format © 1990 Signpost Books Ltd.,
44 Uxbridge Street London W8 7TG
England

Illustrations copyright © 1990 Michael Evans
Text copyright © 1990 Sally Tagholm
Pasteup: Naomi Games
Editor: Dorothy Wood

ISBN 0140 90199 X

Colour separations by Fotographics, Ltd.
Printed and bound in Belgium by Proost Book Production through
Landmark Production Consultants, Ltd.

Typeset by AKM Associates (UK) Ltd, Ajmal House, Hayes Road,
Southall, London

ME

Name: Patrick
Date of birth: 9th April 1981
Time of birth:
Place of birth: Dundee
Weight at birth: 8 ½ p.
Colour of eyes: blue
Colour of hair (if any): blond
Distinguishing marks:

Mum

Dad

Sister/Brother

Sister/Brother

MY FAMILY

January

Thursday January 1
World's biggest bar of chocolate (33.5kg and 1 m long) is auctioned by 'Blue Peter'. It fetches £700.

Friday January 2
Twenty turkeys, chickens and geese are saved from the Christmas oven at Wingshaven Bird Sanctuary in Sussex.

Saturday January 3
Princess Alice of Athlone, the last surviving grandchild of Queen Victoria, dies aged 97.

Sunday January 4
Panther's Comet is named after Roy Panther, who was the first person to spot it from his back garden in Northamptonshire on Christmas night.

Monday January 5
Greece officially celebrates full membership of the European Economic Community.

Tuesday January 6
A dog called Reno is rescued alive 48 days after being buried in an earthquake in southern Italy.   New moon

Wednesday January 7
Biggest shoal of sprats in the Thames Estuary and English Channel for 15 years: the 3000 tonne Russian factory ship *Rudnyy* joins in the catch at Margate.

Thursday January 8
Twenty-seventh London International Boat Show opens at Earl's Court.

Friday January 9
Coal miners in China discover the remains of a woolly mammoth 4.8m high with 3m tusks.

Saturday January 10
The Lord Mayor of London attends the Children's Christmas Fancy Dress Party at the Mansion House 2.30pm.

Sunday January 11
Longest and fastest crossing of Antarctica completed by 3-man British team from the Trans-Globe Expedition. They travelled 4184km in 75 days.

Monday January 12
17,000 entry forms are sent out for the first London Marathon.

Tuesday January 13
Snow! Ice! Roads blocked in the north. 24° frost in Florida. The first snow for 25 years in Tunisia.

Wednesday January 14
Princess Margaret is the first Royal castaway on Desert Island Discs. Her records include 'Rule Britannia' and 'Scotland the Brave'.

January

Named after the Roman god, Janus, who had two faces and could look backwards and forwards at the same time. Also known as 'frosty month', 'wolf month', 'after yule', 'first month' and 'snow month'.

Britain's New Money.

January 27th: Special Announcement from the Chancellor of the Exchequer!

Two new coins are going to be introduced: a £1 coin, the same size as a sovereign, and a 7-sided 20 pence piece. £1 notes, which were introduced just before the First World War, will gradually disappear. Originally they lasted for years but now they only have a life expectancy of about 9 months! This is because the pound is only worth 30 pence compared to its value 10 years ago, so the notes get handled much more. The new £1 coins should last for 40 years!

January weather...

Thick freezing fog over south of England & Wales.

20cm of snow at Glasgow Airport

Gales

Blizzards in the Mediterranean

Oil slick 48km long and 8m wide in the English Channel

Thursday *January 15*	*Gipsy Moth III*, which won the first single-handed transatlantic yacht race, is auctioned for £30,000.
Friday *January 16*	Twenty-year-old Michelle Hobson is crowned Miss Great Britain.
Saturday *January 17*	The Seven Stones Lightship, which marks the reef between Land's End and the Isles of Scilly, breaks her moorings and drifts for 4km.
Sunday *January 18*	RSPB announces that more than 40,000 birds (mainly razor-bills and guillemots) have died in the last twelve months because of oil pollution at sea.
Monday *January 19*	Astronomers in the United States announce the discovery of the largest star ever: it is 3500 times bigger than the Sun and 150,000 light years away.
Tuesday *January 20*	Ronald Reagan is inaugurated as the fortieth President of the United States: at 69, he is the oldest man ever elected. Full Moon
Wednesday *January 21*	Two men, trapped in a diving bell for 10 hours, 121m under the North Sea, are rescued.
Thursday *January 22*	A five-country conference in Oslo decides that the polar bear should remain a protected species. 12°C in London
Friday *January 23*	A cheque written on a crash helmet is accepted by Neath Magistrates' Court, West Glamorgan, in payment of a £15 fine.
Saturday *January 24*	Sonja, an elephant calf weighing 298kg, is stolen from Copenhagen Zoo. Earthquake in S.W. China registers 6.9 on the Richter Scale
Sunday *January 25*	Fifty-two Americans, released after being held hostage in Iran for 14 months, arrive home.
Monday *January 26*	First class letters go up from 12 pence to 14 pence. Second class letters go up from 10 pence to 11½ pence.

Tuesday *January 27*	A plaque is unveiled over a time capsule in Jubilee Gardens, near the Festival Hall, London. It contains such things as the plans for the Thames Barrier, a pictorial history of London and a Tarmac Construction worker's helmet!
Wednesday *January 28*	Coloured dust, probably from the Sahara, rains down over Northern Ireland and Scotland.
Thursday *January 29*	The number of pupils taking school meals has dropped from nearly 5,000,000 a year ago to 3,500,000.
Friday *January 30*	Two cargo ships crash in thick fog at Greenwich at 7.30 pm: *Frederika I* (500 tonnes) sank and the *Blackthorn* (1,173 tonnes) was badly damaged.
Saturday *January 31*	Toy Fair opens at Earl's Court.

Rubbish!

The American hostages, who were held in Iran for fourteen months, were given a huge tickertape parade to welcome them home. Afterwards, more than 1250 tonnes of paper were cleared up! That's more than the Pope got in 1979 (43 tonnes) but not as much as the astronaut, John Glenn, in 1961. He got 3474 tonnes. But the biggest parade ever was to celebrate the victory over Japan in the Second World War in 1945. It produced 5438 tonnes!

Blag 12p

INFLATION FALLS FROM 15.1% TO 13%

DAILY OWL ★

THE BIGGEST YET !!
NEW STAR DIS-COVERED 3,500 TIMES BIGGER THAN THE SUN!

SCANDAL

RECORD TRADE SURPLUS OF £957 MILLION.

The Moon 10p

NATIONAL UNION OF SEAMEN STRIKE.

February

Sunday
February 1

A two-toed sloth is born at Bristol Zoo.

Monday
February 2

The Caxton Young Citizens Awards: Stuart Bell (9), who rescued his disabled mother and baby sister from their blazing home, and Jason Kilby (11), who raised thousands of pounds for Stoke Mandeville Hospital, are joint winners in the youngest age group.

Tuesday
February 3

A hoard of Roman gold and silver, found on a building site near Thetford, Norfolk, is declared Treasure Trove (i.e. it belongs to the Crown).

Wednesday
February 4

Great Dunstan, Canterbury Cathedral's biggest bell (3.5 tonnes), which was cast in 1762, is lowered for repairs.　New Moon

Thursday
February 5

Chinese New Year: The Year of the Rooster!

Friday
February 6

The Post Office issues four new 'Folklore' stamps.

144kph winds at Sumbergh Head, Shetland

Saturday
February 7

First Children's Royal Variety Performance at the London Palladium in aid of the NSPCC.

Gale force winds in the Irish Sea!

Sunday
February 8

Mount St Helens, the volcano which erupted in Washington State last May, is on the boil again.

Monday
February 9

British Rail refreshments go up: a ham sandwich by 2 pence to 46 pence, egg-on-toast by 2 pence to 42 pence and a toasted bacon sandwich by 2 pence to 91 pence.

Tuesday
February 10

There are now 371 robots working in British industry—according to the British Robot Association. There are 6,000 in Japan, 3,500 in the USA, 1,200 in Sweden, 1,133 in Germany and 400 in Italy!

Wednesday
February 11

Tonnes of chalk from the white cliffs of Dover fall into the sea because of heavy rains and frosts.

Thursday
February 12

Long-lost manuscript of a symphony (in F major), which Mozart composed in London when he was 9, has been found in Bavaria.

Friday
February 13

Rupert Murdoch buys *The Times* newspaper.

February

The Roman month of purification. The name comes from the Latin 'februo' which means 'I purify by sacrifice'. It has also been known as 'sprout kale' and 'rain month'.

Year of the Rooster
February 5 1981 – January 24 1982

Chinese horoscopes have nothing to do with western signs of the zodiac. They follow a twelve-year cycle, with each year represented by an animal. According to legend, the Buddha summoned all the animals in the world to him one New Year, promising them a reward. Only twelve obeyed and he gave them each a year, with the first to arrive getting the first year. The order is always the same: the Rat, the Buffalo, the Tiger, the Cat, the Dragon, the Snake, the Horse, the Goat, the Monkey, the Rooster, the Dog and lastly the Pig.

Typical Roosters are dreamers but they speak their minds. They are daring, brave and self-reliant. They like to be noticed and are good company. Active and restless, they work hard and are good at earning money. They are good mates for Buffaloes, Snakes and Dragons but NOT Cats! And watch out if there are two Roosters in the same family.

Royal News Flash!

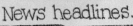

February 24th: The engagement is announced between HRH the Prince of Wales and Lady Diana Spencer. The engagement ring: an oval sapphire, surrounded by 14 diamonds set in 18 carat white gold.

News headlines.

DAILY FISH 15p
POPE VISITS THE PHILIPPINES AND JAPAN.

UNIVERSE 10
FIRST WOMAN 'COX' FOR BOAT RACE TEAM (OXFORD)

The Stamp
FIRST ROUND-THE-WORLD FLIGHT VIA THE SOUTH POLE!

DAILY OCTOPUS 12p
THREE BRITISH MISSIONARIES RELEASED FROM PRISON IN IRAN.

Saturday *February 14*	Irish red setter, Astley's Portia of Rua, wins the Supreme Championship at Crufts.
Sunday *February 15*	The first non-stop round-the-world balloon journey is abandoned. The *Jules Verne* comes down in northern India.
Monday *February 16*	Fishermen blockade the port at Peterhead in protest against cheap foreign fish.
Tuesday *February 17*	Princess Anne is elected Chancellor of London University.
Wednesday *February 18*	A Henry VIII coin, minted in 1526, is sold for £13,000.  Full Moon
Thursday *February 19*	The Zoological Society of London's Stamford Raffles Award goes to Dr E.H. Eason for his work on the classification of centipedes.
Friday *February 20*	US Shuttle *Columbia* tests its engines at Cape Canaveral: 635,040kg of thrust in 20 seconds, held down by eight 91cm bolts!
Saturday *February 21*	International Canoe Exhibition at Crystal Palace National Sports Centre.
Sunday *February 22*	A marathon Monopoly game at Shanklin, Isle of Wight, which lasted 17 days (408 hours) ends at noon, beating the previous record of 388 hours.
Monday *February 23*	10,500 children arrive at the Apollo Theatre, Victoria, to audition for *The Sound of Music*.
Tuesday *February 24*	Opening of the annual Trial of the Pyx at Goldsmith's Hall. A jury of Freemen of the Goldsmith's Company test coins from the Royal Mint to make sure they are the proper weight, diameter and composition.
Wednesday *February 25*	Mr Roland 'Tiny' Rowland to buy the *Observer* newspaper.
Thursday *February 26*	A long-nosed Potoroo (female) is born at London Zoo.
Friday *February 27*	Torquay sea front is closed and the ferry *Scillonian* is stuck in Penzance harbour as gales lash the West Country. Blizzards in Wales — mountain roads are blocked.
Saturday *February 28*	Mr John Winston Ono Lennon of New York leaves estate in England and Wales valued at £2,511,620 net.

UK Fact File 1981

Total area of the United Kingdom 244,090 square kilometres

Capital city

London
(1580 square kilometres;
population 6,696,000)

Population of UK
   Females
   Males

55,676,000
28,626,000
27,050,000

Births

730,900

Marriages

396,900

Deaths

658,000

Most popular girls' name*
Most popular boys' name*

Elizabeth
James

Cub scouts
Brownies

308,000
427,000

Licensed vehicles

19,355,000

Driving Tests

2,031,300 (52.4% failed)

Telephones

27,800,000 (77,000 are
public telephone boxes)

Head of State

Queen Elizabeth II

Prime Minister

Margaret Hilda Thatcher

Members of Parliament

635 (of which 19 are
women)

Poet Laureate

John Betjeman

1981: International Year of the Disabled, Year of the Scot
and Fishermen's Year!

* according to *The Times* newspaper.

March

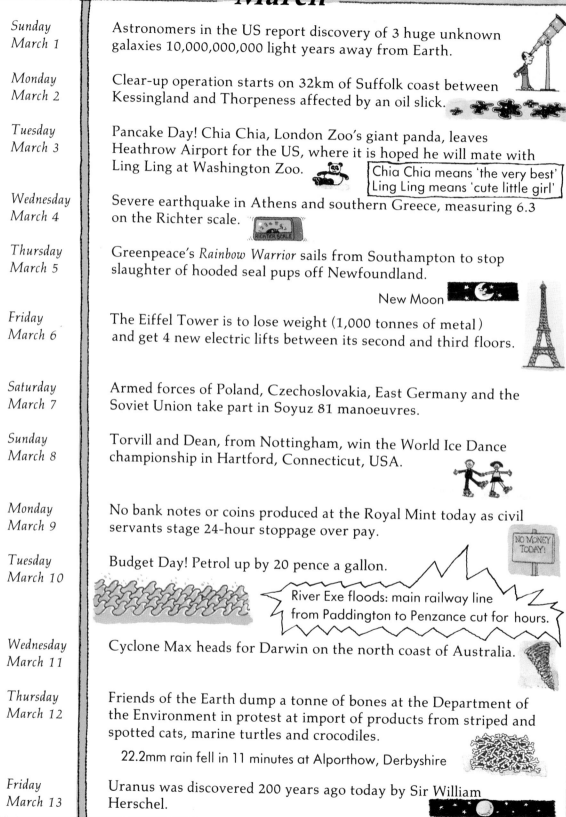

Sunday March 1
Astronomers in the US report discovery of 3 huge unknown galaxies 10,000,000,000 light years away from Earth.

Monday March 2
Clear-up operation starts on 32km of Suffolk coast between Kessingland and Thorpeness affected by an oil slick.

Tuesday March 3
Pancake Day! Chia Chia, London Zoo's giant panda, leaves Heathrow Airport for the US, where it is hoped he will mate with Ling Ling at Washington Zoo.

Chia Chia means 'the very best'
Ling Ling means 'cute little girl'

Wednesday March 4
Severe earthquake in Athens and southern Greece, measuring 6.3 on the Richter scale.

Thursday March 5
Greenpeace's *Rainbow Warrior* sails from Southampton to stop slaughter of hooded seal pups off Newfoundland.

New Moon

Friday March 6
The Eiffel Tower is to lose weight (1,000 tonnes of metal) and get 4 new electric lifts between its second and third floors.

Saturday March 7
Armed forces of Poland, Czechoslovakia, East Germany and the Soviet Union take part in Soyuz 81 manoeuvres.

Sunday March 8
Torvill and Dean, from Nottingham, win the World Ice Dance championship in Hartford, Connecticut, USA.

Monday March 9
No bank notes or coins produced at the Royal Mint today as civil servants stage 24-hour stoppage over pay.

NO MONEY TODAY!

Tuesday March 10
Budget Day! Petrol up by 20 pence a gallon.

River Exe floods: main railway line from Paddington to Penzance cut for hours.

Wednesday March 11
Cyclone Max heads for Darwin on the north coast of Australia.

Thursday March 12
Friends of the Earth dump a tonne of bones at the Department of the Environment in protest at import of products from striped and spotted cats, marine turtles and crocodiles.

22.2mm rain fell in 11 minutes at Alporthow, Derbyshire

Friday March 13
Uranus was discovered 200 years ago today by Sir William Herschel.

March

Named after the Roman God Mars. It has also been known as 'rough-month', 'lengthening month', 'boisterous month' and 'windy month'.

March 25: Stamps for International Year of the Disabled

The First London Marathon

The first London Marathon started in Greenwich Park and was 27.4 metres longer than the official marathon distance of 26 miles 385 yards. The finishing line was in Constitution Hill, by the side of Buckingham Palace, and first across it (hand in hand) were Inge Simonsen (25) of Norway and Dick Beardsley (24) of the USA. Their time was 2 hrs 11.48 mins. The fastest woman was Joyce Smith (43), who finished in 2 hrs 29.56 mins.

Altogether, there were 6700 runners, 1000 volunteer helpers, 500 special constables, 26 first-aid stations and 300 St John Ambulance personnel. There were also 2000 foil blankets, 75 portable lavatories, 400 gallons of coffee and 50,000 plastic cups.

Jimmy Savile wore a gold lamé track suit and collected £50,000 for charity.

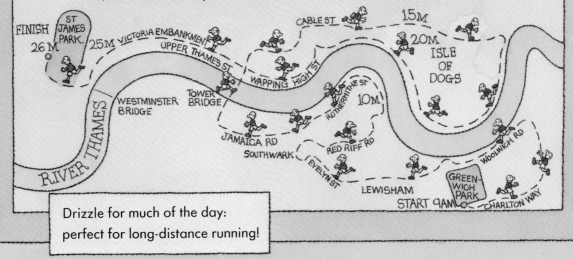

Drizzle for much of the day: perfect for long-distance running!

Saturday March 14th	Twenty-first Football League Cup Final at Wembley: West Ham United and Liverpool draw 1 – 1. (Replay – April 1. Liverpool won 2 – 1.)
Sunday March 15	800 tonne coaster *Amsil* is beached on a sandbank in the Wash, off Hunstanton, Norfolk.
Monday March 16	The Kielder Reservoir, opened in 1980, is filling up: it covers 607 hectares now—by next year, 1011 hectares.
Tuesday March 17	Ching Ching, London Zoo's female giant panda, is taken to University College Hospital for tests.
Wednesday March 18	The Palace Theatre, Manchester, re-opens after a £3,000,000 renovation.
Thursday March 19	Foot and mouth disease breaks out on Jersey.
Friday March 20	Full Moon The Bank of England issues a new £50 note. Spring equinox
Saturday March 21	Tom Baker makes his final appearance as Dr Who.
Sunday March 22	Soviet spaceship *Soyuz 39* is launched to link up with the orbital space lab, *Salyut 6*.
Monday March 23	Isle of Wight sealed off as foot and mouth spreads.
Tuesday March 24	Queen's Park Rangers Football Club are to install a new all-weather surface called 'Omniturf'.
Wednesday March 25	The Post Office issues four new stamps for International Year of the Disabled.
Thursday March 26	The Social Democratic Party is launched by the 'Gang of Four': Roy Jenkins, David Owen, William Rodgers and Shirley Williams.
Friday March 27	The Queen gives her formal consent at a meeting of the Privy Council to the marriage of HRH the Prince of Wales and Lady Diana Spencer. I CONSENT
Saturday March 28	2590 square kilometres of Hampshire, Dorset and the Isle of Wight are cordoned off to prevent the spread of foot and mouth disease.

Heavy rain in Wales and 12cm of snow in Lake District

Sunday March 29	The first London Marathon. British Summer Time starts at 1am —a week later and an hour earlier than usual to bring the UK into line with EEC countries.
Monday March 30	Royal film performance of *Chariots of Fire* in front of the Queen Mother.
Tuesday March 31	A 3 000-year-old Egyptian mummy is unwrapped at Bristol University.

THE NOSY PARKER
We're the nosiest! 9p
PRESIDENT REAGAN IS SHOT AND WOUNDED IN WASHINGTON

SCOOP School girl eats 100 PIES
FLOODS IN SOUTH AFRICA!

DAILY INFO MORE NEWS!
MORE THAN 100 HOSTAGES ON BOARD A HIJACKED PAKISTANI AIRLINER ARE RELEASED.

The Gossip. 10p
MORE THAN 1,000 COYPU (LARGE SOUTH AMERICAN WATER RATS) ARE CAUGHT IN EAST ANGLIA THIS MONTH.

Champions of the Year 1981

Horse of the Year:	Mr Ross (David Broom)
Supreme Champion at Crufts:	Astley's Portia of Rua
Car of the Year:	Ford Escort
Man of the Year:	Prince Charles
Castaway of the Year:	Princess Margaret
Sportsman of the Year:	Sebastian Coe
Sportswoman of the Year:	Jayne Torvill
Lorry Driver of the Year:	Colin Burrows
Pet of the Year:	Goldie (from Blue Peter)
Mastermind:	Leslie Grout
Young Engineers of Great Britain:	John Freeman and Ingram Legge
Times Crossword Champion:	Tony Sever
Children's Book of the Year:	*Fair's Fair* by Leon Garfield
Toy of the Year:	Rubik's Cube
Rubik's Cube Champion:	Julian Chivers
Formula 1 Motor Racing Champion:	Nelson Piquet
Pipeman of the Year:	James Galway
National Brass Band Champions:	Black Dyke Mills Band
Museum of the Year:	National Tractor & Farm Museum in Northumberland

April

Wednesday *April 1*	A pygmy hippo is born at Bristol Zoo. She is called April and weighs approximately 6 kilos. In France an April Fool is called 'un poisson d'avril' and in Scotland a 'gowk' (cuckoo)
Thursday *April 2*	The 73-year old Rotherhithe Tunnel under the river Thames is re-opened after a £2.7 million face-lift.
Friday *April 3*	President Reagan, recovering from the bullet wound in his left lung, has a temperature of 36°C. 25°C in New York New Moon
Saturday *April 4*	Bob Champion wins the Grand National on *Aldaniti*, Oxford wins the Boat Race (coxed by the first woman, Susan Brown) and Bucks Fizz win the Eurovision Song Contest with 'Making Your Mind Up'.
Sunday *April 5*	Census to find out who lives where. The information from 20,000,000 forms will be processed by computers to show population, economic and social trends. The forms are stored in secret for a hundred years and then destroyed!
Monday *April 6*	Start of the 5-day count-down to the launch of the first US space shuttle, *Columbia*.
Tuesday *April 7*	Hundreds of kangaroos wreak havoc in the Australian town of Cobar. Lawns are ruined and cars damaged as the kangaroos search for food after the long drought.
Wednesday *April 8*	Charity premiere of *Superman II* in aid of Special Olympics UK at the Warner Cinema, Leicester Square, London.
Thursday *April 9*	The 175th anniversary of the birth of Isambard Kingdom Brunel, the famous Victorian engineer. A 1.2m cake in the shape of the Clifton Suspension Bridge is made to celebrate! Minor earth tremors 128km north east of Hong Kong measuring between 3.2 and 4.0 on the Richter Scale
Friday *April 10*	Computer problems delay the launch of space shuttle *Columbia* — just half an hour before the scheduled lift-off. Warmest day of the month 22° C in southern England
Saturday *April 11*	Riots in Brixton: 226 people are injured and 196 are arrested.
Sunday *April 12*	US space shuttle *Columbia* finally takes off (1pm British Summer Time — less than 4 secs late) from Cape Canaveral, Florida, USA.

April

The opening month — from the Latin 'aperire' to open. Also known as the time of budding.

Columbia

The US space shuttle, *Columbia*, was the first re-usable space craft. It took 10 years and thousands of millions of dollars to develop. 36m long (about the size of a DC9 jet) it was the first spaceship to have wings and a tail. During its $54\frac{1}{2}$ hour mission, it completed 36 orbits of the earth before re-entering the earth's atmosphere and gliding to a halt on a dry lake bed in the Californian desert. Its top speed in orbit 217 kilometres above earth was 28,163 kph.

The Box Tunnel

April 9 — the only day in the year when the sun is meant to shine right through the Box Tunnel between Bath and Chippenham — all 1.84km of it. It was designed by Brunel (see opposite) and took $2\frac{1}{2}$ years to build. His team worked day and night by the light of candles. They burned 1 tonne of wax, and used 1 tonne of gunpowder every week. It was opened in 1841, but to begin with nervous passengers wouldn't use it because it was so long. They used to get off the train at the station before the tunnel, travel over the hill in horse-drawn carriages, and catch the next train the other side.

Centenary of the Natural History Museum

A special competition was held to design a poster to celebrate the centenary: it was won by Amanda Taylor (14) with a Stegosaurus covered with candles. She became the first mentally handicapped person to win a national art competition.

Lucy Butler won the 8-10 year-old group with a picture of the main entrance of the museum. Her poster was made into greetings cards to sell in the bookshop.

On Centenary Day, April 18 (Easter Saturday), the first 100 children through the doors of the museum were given free tickets to London or Whipsnade Zoos.

There was also a medallion and a special logo for the centenary year.

Happy 100th Birthday Happy 100th Birthday

Happy 100th Birthday Happy 100th Birthday

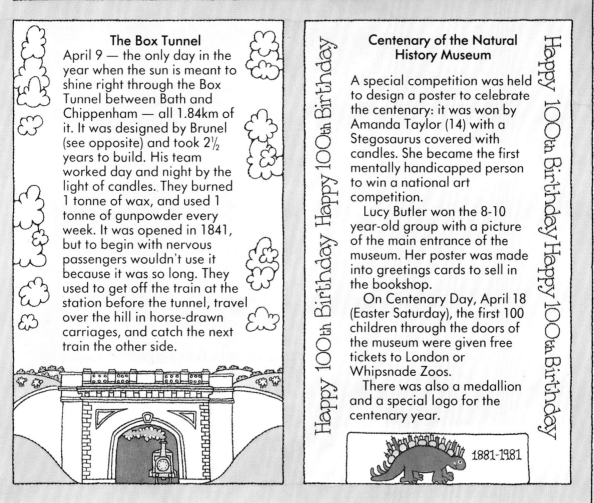

1881-1981

Monday *April 13*	A power failure affects most of London's Underground. Thousands of passengers are stranded in tunnels for up to 80 minutes.
Tuesday *April 14*	Royal Proclamation declaring that July 29th will be a Bank Holiday to mark the marriage of HRH the Prince of Wales and Lady Diana Spencer.
Wednesday *April 15*	Two dolphins arrive at Heathrow Airport from Japan on their way to Liverpool.
Thursday *April 16*	A statue of Charlie Chaplin is unveiled in Leicester Square, London.
Friday *April 17*	Good Friday. Annual Marbles Contest at Battle, Sussex. Opening of the Harcamlow Way footpath from Harlow to Cambridge and back.
Saturday *April 18*	Happy Hundredth Birthday to the Natural History Museum!
Sunday *April 19*	Easter Sunday. Traditional Pace Egging and Egg Rolling ceremonies at Tunbridge Wells, Kent. European Kite Extravaganza 1981 at Blackheath. Full Moon
Monday *April 20*	Steve Davis, (23) wins the world professional snooker title in Sheffield. 'Star Wars' (in 13 parts) starts on Radio 1.
Tuesday *April 21*	The Soviet Union launches *Cosmos-1266*, an unmanned satellite for space research. Queen's birthday.
Wednesday *April 22*	First day of the cricket season. Snow showers in the north and east
Thursday *April 23*	Princess Michael of Kent gives birth to a 3.4kg daughter at St Mary's Paddington: Lady Gabriela Marina Alexandra Ophelia Windsor. −9 C at Carnwath, Strathclyde, Scotland.
Friday *April 24*	Snow in southern Scotland, northern England and Northern Ireland — up to 20cms in places.
Saturday *April 25*	Shakespeare's birthday. Very heavy snow in the Midlands, southern England and the West country. Power lines fall and vehicles stranded.

Sunday *April 26*	A new Scottish newspaper, the *Sunday Standard*, is born in Glasgow, and Little Red Rum (4.8cm high), a miniature Shetland pony, is born at the Children's Zoo in London. More snow and rain in England and Wales
Monday *April 27*	Five air cadets, lost on Dartmoor during the weekend's blizzards, are rescued by the Dartmoor Rescue Group.
Tuesday *April 28*	20,000 homes are still without electricity after the snow brought power lines down at the weekend.
Wednesday *April 29*	A sealed time capsule is placed in the spire of Bedford School at its topping out ceremony (The school burned down two years ago and has been rebuilt). Among other things, it contains a detention form, a boy's tie and a pencil sharpener in the shape of a miniature yellow helmet.
Thursday *April 30*	Locomotive 47712, which operates on the high speed service between Glasgow and Edinburgh, is named *Lady Diana* in a ceremony at Queen Street Station in Glasgow.

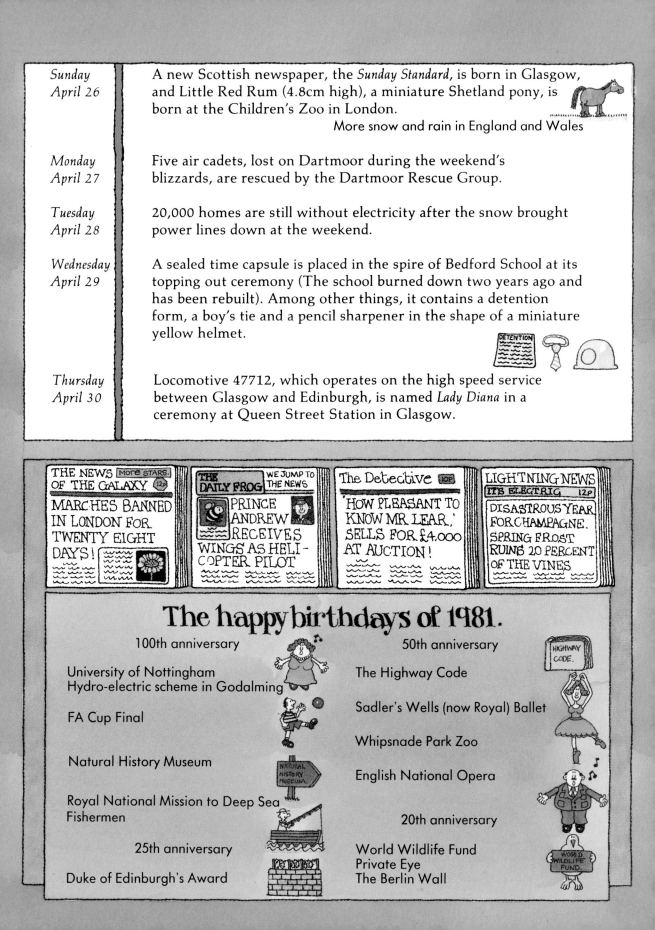

THE NEWS OF THE GALAXY (More Stars) 12p
MARCHES BANNED IN LONDON FOR TWENTY EIGHT DAYS!

THE DAILY FROG — WE JUMP TO THE NEWS
PRINCE ANDREW RECEIVES WINGS AS HELI-COPTER PILOT

The Detective 10p
'HOW PLEASANT TO KNOW MR LEAR,' SELLS FOR £4,000 AT AUCTION!

LIGHTNING NEWS IT'S ELECTRIC 12p
DISASTROUS YEAR FOR CHAMPAGNE. SPRING FROST RUINS 20 PERCENT OF THE VINES

The happy birthdays of 1981.

100th anniversary

University of Nottingham
Hydro-electric scheme in Godalming

FA Cup Final

Natural History Museum

Royal National Mission to Deep Sea Fishermen

25th anniversary

Duke of Edinburgh's Award

50th anniversary

The Highway Code

Sadler's Wells (now Royal) Ballet

Whipsnade Park Zoo

English National Opera

20th anniversary

World Wildlife Fund
Private Eye
The Berlin Wall

May

Friday *May 1*	The Empire State Building is 50 years old! All 381m, 102 floors and 6500 windows of it!
Saturday *May 2*	An Aer Lingus Boeing 737 jet is hijacked between Dublin and London by an ex-Trappist monk and forced to land in France.
Sunday *May 3*	Cromer Zoo is for sale—asking price £75,000, including animals. The owner is the daughter of Coco the clown, who opened it 20 years ago. New Moon Snow, hail & thunder!
Monday *May 4*	Bank Holiday. 12,000 people hold hands to make a 16km circle round Wrekin Hill, near Telford, Shropshire.
Tuesday *May 5*	The Queen and the Duke of Edinburgh begin a 4-day state visit to Norway.
Wednesday *May 6*	Cannibal fish called Zander have been eating native fish in the Cambridgeshire fens. Introduced in 1963 from Eastern Europe, anglers have killed off more than 3 tonnes of them in a massive cull.
Thursday *May 7*	Canadian Indians smoke peace pipes in Parliament Square: they are petitioning Mrs Thatcher, MPs and the Queen about their land rights.
Friday *May 8*	Prince Andrew Alexandrovitch of Russia, grandson of Tsar Alexander III and nephew of Tsar Nicholas II, dies in Kent aged 84.
Saturday *May 9*	Hundreth FA Cup Final at Wembley: Tottenham Hotspur and Manchester City draw 1-1 in front of a crowd of 99,500.
Sunday *May 10*	Stunt motor bike rider Ellie Taylor breaks a woman's world record by jumping 15.24m over 5 single-decker buses at Lilford Park, Northamptonshire. She also breaks her nose!
Monday *May 11*	'CATS' opens at the New London Theatre, Drury Lane.
Tuesday *May 12*	National Campaign to Save the British Butterfly is launched by David Bellamy.
Wednesday *May 13*	The Duke of Gloucester unveils a headstone in Greyfriars Church, Edinburgh. It says: 'Greyfriars Bobby died 1872 aged 16. Let his loyalty and devotion be a lesson to us all.'
Thursday *May 14*	FA Cup Final replay at Wembley: Tottenham Hotspur beats Manchester City 3–2.
Friday *May 15*	Princess Anne gives birth to a 4.34kg daughter at St Mary's, Paddington: Zara Anne Elizabeth Phillips (8.15pm).

May

The Dutch called it 'Bloumaand' which means blossoming month.

Takes its name from Maia, the goddess of growth and increase.

May 1st — May 7th: Empire State Building Week in New York

The Empire State Building cost $12,000,000 to build and 10,000,000 bricks were used. It has 61 passenger lifts and 6 goods lifts. It has its own fire brigade, police force and post office. In a 160 kph wind it bends 3.8cm. In 1945, a B-25 bomber crashed into the 79th floor, killing the crew and 11 people in the building. Every year there is a race to the top!

14p Small Tortoiseshell

18p Large Blue

22p Peacock

25p Chequered Skipper

Butterfly Stamps
May 13

Greyfriars Bobby

Greyfriars Bobby was a Skye Terrier, who guarded his master's grave for 14 years. He was given the freedom of the city of Edinburgh by the Lord Provost and, more recently, Walt Disney made a film about him. He was buried next to his master, John Gray, and there is a statue of him on the George IV Bridge in Edinburgh.

Whipsnade Park Zoo

Whipsnade was the first open-country zoo. It was set up to keep animals in natural conditions and for breeding purposes. After 50 years, about 85 percent of the mammals and 60 percent of the birds at the park are born there. In fact, it has one of the best records in Europe for breeding wild animals in captivity. As well as Przewalski's horse and Père David's deer, cheetahs have been particularly successful. The Queen is sometimes given animals by foreign leaders and some are kept at Whipsnade. In the past 10 years she has been given 2 jaguars, 2 giant ant-eaters, 1 giant armadillo, 1 two-toed sloth, 6 toucans, 6 red kangaroos, 1 bare-eyed cockatoo, 1 white donkey and 1 African elephant.

Saturday May 16	Four hundred teams set out on the Ten Tors Expedition on Dartmoor. They have to complete 56km, 72km or 88km in 34hrs (according to age) with a 10-hour stop at night.
Sunday May 17	Eight hundred walkers drop out of the Ten Tors Expedition because of heavy rain, thick mist and high winds!
Monday May 18	The Queen visits the sixtieth Chelsea Flower Show. Full Moon
Tuesday May 19	Twenty-fifth anniversary of the Victoria and George Cross Association: 13 Victoria Cross holders and 34 George Cross holders celebrate at the Imperial War Museum.
Wednesday May 20	Mrs Enid Hattersley is installed Lord Mayor of Sheffield (the sixth woman to hold the office). She is the mother of Roy Hattersley, Labour spokesman on home affairs.
Thursday May 21	The Janacek Suite is played at the wrong speed, 45 rpm instead, of 33 rpm, on Radio Three this morning!
Friday May 22	The annual Devon Show is almost washed away by torrential rain: 3,000 tonnes of limestone is brought from a near-by quarry to save the day!
Saturday May 23	Happy Birthday Whipsnade Park Zoo! To celebrate its fiftieth year, visitors are admitted at the equivalent 1931 prices of five pence for an adult and twopence ha'penny for a child. A wet and cold Bank Holiday weekend!
Sunday May 24	The Milk Bike Race starts in Brighton 15° C in London
Monday May 25	Bank Holiday. Three Snowy Owls are hatched at London Zoo. Man dressed as Spiderman climbs the world's tallest building—the 443m Sears Tower in Chicago. It took him 6½ hours.
Tuesday May 26	Two Soviet cosmonauts return to earth after 75 days in space.
Wednesday May 27	A new permanent exhibition, 'The Origin of the Species', opens at the Natural History Museum.
Thursday May 28	General Perky, the Imperial War Museum's official cat, who is well past retirement age, is given 'an extended unpaid appointment with non-pensionable emoluments or free board and lodgings within the museum'.

Friday *May 29*	Competition in Battersea Park to find Britain's strongest man: 127kg Dick Slaney lifts 10 girls on a steel girder—total weight 997kg!
Saturday *May 30*	For Sale: Billingsgate Fish Market
	Fruit is damaged by cold, wet, windy weather
Sunday *May 31*	Five hundred people arrive in Trafalgar Square, London, at the end of the People's March for Jobs, which set off from Liverpool on May 1 (450km).

Top Tens of the Year 1981

Top Ten Singles
(according to *NME*)
1. Vienna (Ultravox)
2. Ghost Town (Specials)
3. Tainted Love (Soft Cell)
4. This Old House (Shakin' Stevens)
5. Stand and Deliver (Adam and the Ants)
6. Imagine (John Lennon)
7. One Day In Your Life (Michael Jackson)
8. Antmusic (Adam and the Ants)
9. Being With You (Smokey Robinson)
10. Prince Charming (Adam and the Ants)

Top Ten Singles Artists
(according to *NME*)
1. Adam and the Ants
2. Shakin' Stevens
3. John Lennon
4. Madness
5. Ultravox
6. Toyah
7. Kim Wilde
8. Human League
9. Stevie Wonder
10. The Police

Top Ten Names (girls)
(according to *The Times*)
1. Elizabeth
2. Louise
3. Jane
4. Sarah
5. Charlotte
6. Victoria
7. Mary
8. Katherine
9. Alexandra
10. Lucy

Top Ten Names (boys)
(according to *The Times*)
1. James
2. William
3. Alexander
4. Thomas
5. Edward
6. John
7. Charles
8. David
9. Nicholas
10. Michael

Top Ten Films
(according to *Screen International*)
1. Superman II
2. For Your Eyes Only
3. Flash Gordon
4. Snow White and the Seven Dwarfs
5. Any Which Way You Can
6. Clash of the Titans
7. Private Benjamin
8. Raiders of the Lost Ark
9. The Elephant Man
10. Tess

Top Ten Toys
1. Rubik's Cube
2. Star Wars
3. Cindy
4. Lego
5. Astro Wars
6. Action Man
7. Rubik's Snake
8. Connect 4
9. Britain's Farm Animals and Space Toys
10. The Kensington Game

June

Monday *June 1*	Rain swamps the world gliding championships in Germany.
Tuesday *June 2*	The 19,500 tonne anti-submarine carrier *Ark Royal* is launched by the Queen Mother on the Tyne. It's the fifth British warship to have this name since the Spanish Armada in 1588. **New Moon**
Wednesday *June 3*	*Shergar*, ridden by 19-year-old Walter Swinburn, wins the Derby at Epsom.
Thursday *June 4*	A survey in *Which?* magazine says that mice prefer chocolate, dried fruit, nuts or lard in their traps, not cheese!
Friday *June 5*	Rare sighting of the river warbler at Roydon in west Norfolk. Only the fifth time it has been seen in Britain—it usually lives in eastern Europe.
Saturday *June 6*	World's first test-tube twins (a boy and a girl) born at Queen Victoria Hospital in Melbourne, Australia.
Sunday *June 7*	Whit Sunday. A 1448km pilgrimage for peace which left Iona, Argyll, on Good Friday, arrives in Canterbury.
Monday *June 8*	Bank Holiday. The Trimaran *Bonifacio* capsizes 563km west of Land's End in the *Observer* Transatlantic Race. The crew is rescued by a Royal Navy helicopter.
Tuesday *June 9*	Hundreds of thousands of seals are invading Norway's fishing grounds. George Stephenson, who invented the railway engine, was born 200 years ago.
Wednesday *June 10*	Sebastian Coe breaks his own 800m world record by more than half a second in Florence. His time of 1 min 41.72 secs still stands.
Thursday *June 11*	The Queen opens Britain's tallest office building, the National Westminster Tower in the City of London (182.9m).
Friday *June 12*	Norman Croucher from London, who has two artificial legs, reaches the top of White Needle Peak (6539.2m) in the Himalayas.
Saturday *June 13*	Six blank shots are fired at the Queen as she rides from Buckingham Palace to Horseguards Parade for the Trooping the Colour ceremony.
Sunday *June 14*	A 181.6kg 4m-long shark leaps at a small fishing boat, the *Albatross*, off the Isle of Wight and lands across the deck.
Monday *June 15*	Beware of strange bobbing objects on the south coast: three canisters have been washed ashore at Christchurch and Bournemouth containing a liquid which has an effect like nerve gas.

June

Probably took its name from the Latin 'Juniores', which means young people, who were honoured at this time of year. Or did it come from the great goddess Juno?

The old Anglo-Saxon name was 'Seremonath' (dry month) or 'Lida serra' (joy month)

An old French name was 'Prairial' (meadow month)

Breeders at the National Vegetable Research station near Warwick, have been trying to grow a British baked bean for 8 years! One that will survive the weather and be the right shape, size, colour, and texture–just like the ones we import from the USA. So far they have tried 720 different varieties and have still not found the perfect British Baked Bean!

The great raft spider is Britain's largest and rarest spider. It was only discovered in 1956. Between 7–10cm in diameter, it has a brown or black velvet body with white flashes down the sides and fleshy legs.

Sebastian Coe set some other important world records in 1981: the 1000m in 2 mins 12.18 secs and the mile in 3 mins 47.33 secs.

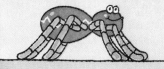

A record-setting 3.2km sausage was made by Dewhurst Butchers for the Great Children's Party in Hyde Park in 1979. On Saturday, June 27, 1981, the record was broken by a sausage in Aix-en-Provence, France. It measured 4.3km. On Sunday, June 28, 1981, a new world record was set in Le Mans by another French sausage. It measured 4.7km!

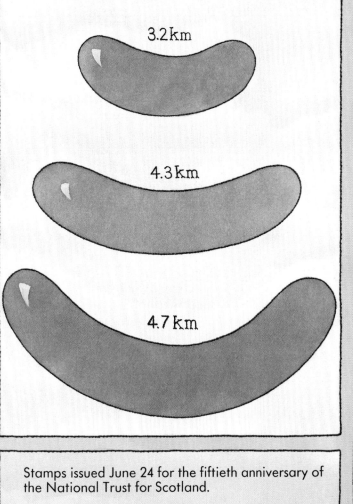

3.2km

4.3km

4.7km

Stamps issued June 24 for the fiftieth anniversary of the National Trust for Scotland.

Tuesday June 16	*Solar Challenger*, the first solar-cell powered aircraft, makes a successful 2½ hour test flight, reaching 1524m at a maximum speed of 67.6kph.
Wednesday June 17	Two-seater aircraft, *The Spirit of Truro*, built by the pupils of Truro School, makes its first official flight. It cost £4000 to build and is powered by a Volkswagen car engine.

Full Moon

Thursday June 18	The 147.2m-long white lion on the Downs at Whipsnade Park Zoo in Bedfordshire is given a new wooden eye and is cleaned up with 80 tonnes of chalk.
Friday June 19	Twenty-nine Odeon and Gaumont cinemas are to close: 13 in London and others in Aldershot, Ashton, Bury, Canterbury, Cardiff, Chelmsford, Chesterfield, Darlington, Dundee, Eglinton Toll (Glasgow), Hartlepool, Lincoln, Rochester, Sale, Stafford and Stockton.

High pollen count of 72

Saturday June 20	The twenty-fifth anniversary of the Duke of Edinburgh's Gold Award Scheme is marked by a race from Selfridge's in Oxford Street, London, to Calais and back: five teams of celebrities start at 9am.
Sunday June 21	The longest day of the year. The summer solstice is celebrated at Stonehenge. Chay Blythe and Rob James win the *Observer* Transatlantic Yacht race in 14 days 13 hrs and 54 mins.
Monday June 22	Prince Charles dives to the wreck of the Tudor warship *Mary Rose* which capsized in 1545, 1.6km off Portsmouth Harbour.

First day of the Wimbledon Tennis Championship

Tuesday June 23	The Duchess of Gloucester is presented with a single red rose by the pupils of the village school in Barnwell, Northamptonshire, as a token rent, according to a seventeenth-century custom.
Wednesday June 24	Lady Donaldson is elected the first woman Sheriff of the City of London. The first traffic moves across the Humber Bridge after its informal opening. New stamps!

Rain at Wimbledon
Drought in East Kent

Thursday June 25	The sixty-eighth *Tour de France* starts in Nice. Fun Ride in Hyde Park, London to mark the launch of national Ride-a-Bike Week on Sunday.

Friday *June 26*	The Design Council unveils 60 selected souvenirs for the Royal Wedding. They include a red, white and blue rosette with red flashing lights, a mug with a handle in the shape of Prince Charles's ear, and a tea cosy that looks like a crown.
Saturday *June 27*	Annual Open Day at the National Vegetable Research Station, Warwick, where they are trying to breed a British baked bean.
Sunday *June 28*	*Voyager 2*, which was launched in August 1977, sends back its first photographs of Saturn. Great raft spider hunt at Redgrave and Lopham Reserve in Suffolk.
	Only 592 hours of sunshine so far this year!
Monday *June 29*	Widespread frost. The fourth coldest June for 20 years.
Tuesday *June 30*	The last minute of June has 61 seconds in it this year to bring the Earth's clock and the atomic clock into line.

Assorted Royal Wedding Souvenirs

Flashing red, white and blue rosette

Thimble

Mug

Tea cosy

Plastic union jack football rattle decorated with Charles and Diana, 45p

Silver-mounted pincushion, £75

Slate Paperweight, £13.50

Scrap book, 11p

Daily Bleet 12p
POPE DISCHARGED FROM HOSPITAL

GRAPEVINE. 10p
DR. GARRETT FITZGERALD BECOMES PRIME MINISTER OF THE IRISH REPUBLIC.

THE DAILY BLURB.
GOON KNIGHTED IN QUEEN'S BIRTHDAY HONOURS LIST- NOW SIR HARRY SECOMBE!

PUFF. 14p
KING KHALID OF SAUDI ARABIA ARRIVES ON THREE-DAY STATE VISIT.

July

Wednesday *July 1*	Happy birthday, Lady Diana! — 20 today. New penguin pool opened at Chester Zoo by Patrick Moore. He composed and played a special tune 'Playful Penguin' on the xylophone accompanied by the Upton High School Band. New Moon
Thursday *July 2*	The *Trafalgar* (4500 tonnes), the first in a new class of 6 Fleet nuclear-powered submarines, is launched at Barrow-in-Furness Tropical storms in the Philippines kill 145 people
Friday *July 3*	Chris Evert-Lloyd (USA) wins her third Wimbledon single's title, beating Hana Mandlikova 6-2, 6-2.
Saturday *July 4*	John McEnroe (USA) wins his first Wimbledon single's title, beating Bjorn Borg 4-6, 7-6, 7-6, 6-4.
Sunday *July 5*	Opening service for the Festival of the City of London at St. Paul's Cathedral, 11am.
Monday *July 6*	Justin Frost (12) who won a painting competition, stands on his head at the National Portrait Gallery in London: his painting was hung upside down.
Tuesday *July 7*	The solar-powered flying machine *Solar Challenger* flies across the English Channel, completing the 289km journey from Paris to Manston in Kent in $5\frac{1}{2}$ hours at a cruising speed of 59kph. A crown worth 25 pence, is issued to commemorate the Royal Wedding.
Wednesday *July 8*	A 7.6cm lead model of Henry V on a charger fetches £130 at a toy sale in London—a world record for a single lead figure.
Thursday *July 9*	The National Chess Championship is won by St Paul's School. The average age of the team is 15. Worst storms for six years. A woman is struck by lightning in Somerset. The London Weather Centre records 5cm of rain between 3 and 4pm.
Friday *July 10*	Huge firework display at Goodwood Racecourse as part of the Chichester 906 festivities.
Saturday *July 11*	Fifty Tiger Moth planes fly from Hatfield, Bristol, to RAF station at Cranwell, Lincolnshire to mark the 50 years since the first Tiger Moth was produced.
Sunday *July 12*	London taxi fares rise by 13 per cent. The 50p minimum fare will cover the first 647m or 3 mins 36 secs. Then the rate will be 10p for each 323.5m or 1 min 48 secs. After that it's 10p for each 215.7m or 1 min 12 secs.

July

Named in honour of Julius Caesar

The Saxons called it 'Maedd-Monath' because it was when the cattle were turned into the meadows to feed.

The Dutch called it 'Hooy-maand' — hay month.

Royal wedding stamps issued.

The Royal Wedding

The time: 11 am Wednesday July 29th, 1981.
The place: St Paul's Cathedral, London.
The happy HRH the Prince of Wales and
couple: Lady Diana Spencer.
The guests: 2,500 (assorted) including the King of Norway, the Queen of Denmark, the King and Queen of Sweden, the Queen of the Netherlands, the Grand Duke and Duchess of Luxembourg, the Prince and Princess of Liechtenstein and Princess Grace of Monaco.

The bridesmaids: Lady Sarah Armstrong-Jones, Miss India Hicks, Miss Catherine Cameron, Miss Sarah Jane Gaselee and Miss Clementine Hambro.
The pages: Lord Nicholas Windsor and Mr Edward van Cutsem.
The dress: Ivory pure silk taffeta and old lace, embroidered with tiny mother of pearl sequins and pearls, with a 7.6m train.
Flowers: Bouquet of gardenias, golden Mountbatten roses, lily-of-the-valley and white freesias with a cascade of white odontoglossum orchids and stephanotis.

THE LOUD HAILER 12p
THE WORLD GOES TO A WEDDING; CHARLES AND DI TIE THE KNOT.

DAILY SCRIBBLE 10p
SUPERBRAT TAKES OVER THE WIMBLEDON CROWN.

BATTY 15p
QUEEN COUNTS HER SWANS.

THE DAILY SHOUT.
MAN JUMPS FROM BLOCK OF FLATS TO AID HOSPITAL.

Monday *July 13*	Swan-upping starts on the river Thames with the Royal Keeper of the Swans, Captain John Turk.
Tuesday *July 14*	French yachtsman Marc Pajot completes the 4707-km crossing from New York to the Lizard in Cornwall in 9 days 10 hrs 6 mins, beating the record by more than 19 hrs.
Wednesday *July 15*	One-hundred-and-first Royal Tournament starts at Earl's Court.
Thursday *July 16*	New concrete pier, 304.8m long, is opened at Bournemouth.
Friday *July 17*	The new Humber suspension bridge (2200m long) is opened by the Queen at 10.30am. Full Moon
Saturday *July 18*	Mel Harvey jumps 38.1m from the top of a block of flats in Hatfield, Herts, on to a 3m pile of cardboard boxes in aid of the Queen Elizabeth II Hospital in Welwyn Garden City.
Sunday *July 19*	Save the Whale rally in Hyde Park organized by Friends of the Earth. Heavy snow in the French Alps—10 mountain passes are closed. Twenty boy scouts are rescued after 17 hrs.
Monday *July 20*	Royal International Horse Show at Wembley. International Whaling Commission meeting starts in Brighton.
Tuesday *July 21*	Monty, a 3.3m 2-year-old giraffe moves home. He travels in a crate on a low loader from Regent's Park to Whipsnade.
Wednesday *July 22*	The last three keepers leave the Eddystone Lighthouse by helicopter. The lights were switched off yesterday for a year while it is being automated.
	Royal wedding stamps issued.
Thursday *July 23*	The search for the *Titanic*, which sank in 1919 in the north Atlantic, is given up. The expedition's leader has already looked for Noah's Ark on Mount Ararat, and for Pancho Villa's treasure in Mexico.
Friday *July 24*	A record 10 greater flamingo chicks have hatched at Slimbridge Wildfowl Trust, Gloucestershire this season.
Saturday *July 25*	Topping out ceremony at Leeds Castle, Kent: 76.2m of the wall of the moat has been restored.
Sunday *July 26*	5000 children at 861 tables consume 10 tonnes of food and drink at the longest street party to celebrate the royal wedding; it runs along Oxford Street from Tottenham Court Road to Portman Place.

Monday *July 27*	Telephone cards are tried out for the first time at some London railway stations. Crowds begin to camp out along the route of the wedding procession to be sure of a good view.
Tuesday *July 28*	£80,000 firework display in Hyde Park. The Prince of Wales lights the first of 102 beacons and bonfires spread across the country.

Major earthquake in Iran, 7.3 on the Richter Scale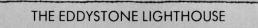

Wednesday *July 29*	The wedding of the Prince of Wales and Lady Diana Spencer takes place at 11am in St. Paul's Cathedral. Bank holiday!
Thursday *July 30*	A satellite breaks up shortly after midnight—according to a research unit at Aston University, Birmingham.

New Moon — the second this month!

Friday *July 31*	Sponsor a minute of diving time from the Mary Rose Trust, which hopes to raise £1,500,000 towards recovering the warship. £1 per minute.

THE EDDYSTONE LIGHTHOUSE
built on a small and very dangerous rock about 21 km from Plymouth

Number one was built in 1698 and just survived its first winter.

Number two (1699–1703) was destroyed in the worst storm ever recorded

Number three (1709–1755) caught fire, burned for five days and was completely destroyed

Number four built in 1759, was made of quick-drying cement and granite.

In the 1870's cracks appeared in the rock, so the top was taken off

and re-erected on Plymouth Hoe

Number five, the present lighthouse, was built in 1882

In 1980, modernisation began, and a helideck was installed

1981, the last keepers leave as the lighthouse goes automatic.

Facts:
Height: 51m
Range: 38.6km
Intensity: 570,000
            candlepower
Characteristics:
white group flashing
twice every 10 secs.

Weather in July

Worst floods for 75 years in China; the Yangtse River bursts its banks and at least 3000 people are reported killed. Floods in India

August

Saturday *August 1*	Prince Charles and Lady Diana (the Prince and Princess of Wales) set off on their honeymoon cruise from Gibraltar — accompanied by a school of dolphins.
Sunday *August 2*	New British record set by human-powered supertrike 'Poppy Flyer 11½' at Greenham Common in Berkshire. Postman Steve Poulter pedals to 76.26kph!
Monday *August 3*	The pleasure steamer *Prince Ivanhoe* hits the rocks off Port Eynon on the Gower Peninsula, South Wales.
Tuesday *August 4*	Hot and sunny! The warmest place is Finningley, south Yorkshire, 29°C, the sunniest Aberdeen with 13.9 hours. 28°C in London.
Wednesday *August 5*	Opening of the exhibition of 1200 royal wedding gifts at St. James's Palace. About 3500 people visit on the first day in temperatures of nearly 30°C.
Thursday *August 6*	The London Fire Brigade on full flood alert after violent storms, and 4.5cm of rain between 9am and 2pm. One carriageway of the Blackwall Tunnel is closed.
Friday *August 7*	The Egton Bridge Gooseberry Show, Yorkshire has been held in the first week of August since 1800. This year, Harry Smith's Yellow Gooseberry goes into the official record books at 25 drams 14 grains.
Saturday *August 8*	The world snake sit-in record is challenged by John Berry, who plans to spend the next 10 days with 24 poisonous snakes in a 3.5sq m cage at Dudley Zoo.
Sunday *August 9*	Three tonnes of fish fall off a lorry along 6km of the Harrogate to York road.
Monday *August 10*	Mrs. Thatcher, on holiday in Cornwall, climbs down 60.9m and 125 steps to the beach at Bedruthan, near Newquay.
Tuesday *August 11*	The official BBC record album of the royal wedding goes to No. 1 in the LP charts. Gary the Zebra is born to Mary and Jeff at London Zoo.
Wednesday *August 12*	The royal yacht *Britannia*, with the Prince and Princess of Wales aboard, drops anchor at Port Said, Egypt.
Thursday *August 13*	Jon Erikson (USA) becomes the first person to swim the Channel three ways. He first swam it when he was 14 years old. His father, Ted, twice swam it both ways!

Friday *August 14*	A capybara, which escaped from London Zoo, spends the day at large before returning to the gate of its paddock to be let in. Its mate is still missing.
Saturday *August 15*	Happy Birthday to Princess Anne. Napoleon Bonaparte would have been 212 today (born 1769).
Sunday *August 16*	International Birdman Rally at Bognor Regis: 50 people splash off the end of the pier trying to fly 50m to win £3000.00. The best attempt (which wins the £300 consolation prize) is 13m.
Monday *August 17*	England retain the Ashes after the fifth Test Match at Old Trafford. Ian Botham named 'Man of the Match' for the third time running

> Bill Neal paddles across the Channel in a bath in 13 hrs 29 mins.

Tuesday *August 18*	Ruth Lawrence (10) has passed her 'A' level in pure maths with an A grade! She's never been to school, but has been taught at home in Huddersfield by her parents.
Wednesday *August 19*	Sebastian Coe regains the world mile record from Steve Ovett in Zurich, Switzerland, with a time of 3 mins 48.53 secs.

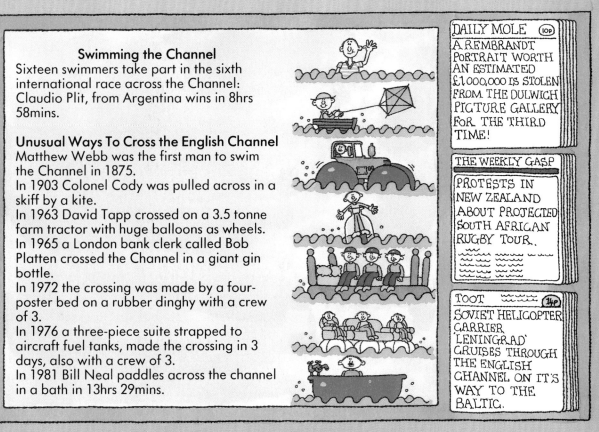

Swimming the Channel
Sixteen swimmers take part in the sixth international race across the Channel: Claudio Plit, from Argentina wins in 8hrs 58mins.

Unusual Ways To Cross the English Channel
Matthew Webb was the first man to swim the Channel in 1875.
In 1903 Colonel Cody was pulled across in a skiff by a kite.
In 1963 David Tapp crossed on a 3.5 tonne farm tractor with huge balloons as wheels.
In 1965 a London bank clerk called Bob Platten crossed the Channel in a giant gin bottle.
In 1972 the crossing was made by a four-poster bed on a rubber dinghy with a crew of 3.
In 1976 a three-piece suite strapped to aircraft fuel tanks, made the crossing in 3 days, also with a crew of 3.
In 1981 Bill Neal paddles across the channel in a bath in 13hrs 29mins.

DAILY MOLE (10p)
A REMBRANDT PORTRAIT WORTH AN ESTIMATED £1,000,000 IS STOLEN FROM THE DULWICH PICTURE GALLERY FOR THE THIRD TIME!

THE WEEKLY GASP
PROTESTS IN NEW ZEALAND ABOUT PROJECTED SOUTH AFRICAN RUGBY TOUR.

TOOT (14p)
SOVIET HELICOPTER CARRIER 'LENINGRAD' CRUISES THROUGH THE ENGLISH CHANNEL ON IT'S WAY TO THE BALTIC.

Thursday *August 20*	Officials announce delay of the second launch of the US space shuttle *Columbia* (due on September 30) because of complications with the rocket boosters.
Friday *August 21*	More than 100 dinosaur footprints have been found on a building site between 2 houses in Swanage, Dorset, 400m from the sea. Experts say they were made by *Meglosauruses*.
Saturday *August 22*	Julian Nott becomes the first person to cross the Channel in a solar-powered balloon: he takes 75 minutes to cross from South Barham, nr. Canterbury, to St. Inglevert, nr. Calais.
Sunday *August 23*	Europe's biggest marathon, with 8700 runners, from Bolton to Manchester and back, is won by Stanley Curran from Middleton, nr. Manchester. His time: 2 hrs, 19 mins. It's also his thirty-fourth birthday!
Monday *August 24*	Exhibition at the Commonwealth Institute includes the third largest star sapphire in the world. It is guarded by a cobra in the same showcase!
Tuesday *August 25*	*Voyager 2* approaches Saturn: it records a series of strange hums and whistles that are emitted by Saturn's rings and moons.
Wednesday *August 26*	*Voyager 2* is at its closest to Saturn (101,388.4 km). It sends back pictures of Hyperion, the eighth largest of Saturn's seventeen known moons—it looks like a battered potato! Steve Ovett wins back the mile record from Sebastian Coe in Koblenz with a time of 3 mins 48.40 secs.
Thursday *August 27*	Anne-France Rix (8) from Upper Poppleton nr. York, is the youngest winner of the Post Office's 1981 National Letter Writing Competition.
Friday *August 28*	Sebastian Coe takes the mile record back from Steve Ovett again in Brussels, with a time of 3 mins 47.33 secs.
Saturday *August 29*	Twenty-eight yachts leave Portsmouth at the start of the 41,842km Round-the-World Yacht Race. New Moon
Sunday *August 30*	Celebrity teddy bears attend the Bears' Bank Holiday at Longleat in Wiltshire. *Winnie the Pooh* is read in Latin. Mrs. Thatcher's teddy bear wears blue dungarees.
Monday *August 31*	Bank Holiday. DO NOT DISTURB notices outside Ching Ching's cage at London Zoo. She is believed to be pregnant and the crowds are gathering.

September

Tuesday *September 1*	Petrol pumps go metric! From today prices are marked in litres as well as gallons. **2 oil slicks off north Northumberland coast near Farne Islands bird sanctuary**
Wednesday *September 2*	US space shuttle *Columbia* travels at 1kph towards the launch pad at Kennedy Space Centre in Florida for the second time this year. It uses 4 litres of fuel every 5 metres!
Thursday *September 3*	A glass fibre statue of John Lennon called 'Working Class Hero' is put on show in Mathew Street, Liverpool.
Friday *September 4*	Winning poster in Superman's campaign against Nick O'Teen, sponsored by the Health Education Council, is designed by Keeley Harrison (10) from Melton Mowbray, Leicestershire. **Earthquake in Southern California 5.8 on Richter Scale**
Saturday *September 5*	The Stackpole Reserve, about 202 hectares of coastline in south Pembrokeshire, becomes a nature reserve. **Floods in China kill over 700 people**
Sunday *September 6*	Beginning of the oyster season! Dave Grylls (23) from San Diego in California, wins the Aspro Clear Speed Challenge road race for human-powered vehicles at Goodwood in 59 mins 57 secs.
Monday *September 7*	Hurricane Floyd races towards Bermuda: winds gust up to 110 knots.
Tuesday *September 8*	Invasion of poisonous-spined weever fish at Saunton and Croyde in North Devon.
Wednesday *September 9*	John Fritzsch (42) from Barnet, Hertfordshire, fails in his attempt to windsurf non-stop from Britain to Holland: he is becalmed 19km out of Felixstowe.
Thursday *September 10*	Twenty-two children from the St John Houghton Roman Catholic School in Kirk Hallam, Derbyshire, start a 2092km relay run to Rome.
Friday *September 11*	Daphne, 21-years-old, is the only pelican left in St. James Park!
Saturday *September 12*	Japanese seaweed is creeping along the Cornish Coast! It has been found off Polperro and Sennen.
Sunday *September 13*	Horseman's Sunday: horses and riders take part in an open-air service at Tattenham Corner, Epsom Downs.

Monday *September 14*	Bargemen spot Wally, a half-tonne walrus from the Arctic at the mouth of the Wash. Full Moon
Tuesday *September 15*	Wally is sighted again—this time in the river Ouse at Salters Lode.
Wednesday *September 16*	Hamleys, the biggest toy shop in the world, moves two doors down in Regent Street, London, to bigger premises!
Thursday *September 17*	Dinky the dolphin is born, tail first, at Windsor Safari Park in front of a crowd of 60!
Friday *September 18*	The French National Assembly abolish capital punishment.
Saturday *September 19*	Thamesday on the river Thames in London. The Egremont Crab Fair in Cumbria. Violent storms with winds up to 128kph—life boats are called out 25 times. An Icelandic coaster sinks 25km off Land's End in hurricane force 12.
Sunday *September 20*	Passengers on a Dunkirk to Ramsgate ferry are stranded in the Channel all night, unable to get into harbour.
Monday *September 21*	The Thames TV London-to-Paris balloon race does not take place because the winds are in the wrong direction this week! FOR SALE: LAND'S END
Tuesday *September 22*	Wally the walrus flops onto the beach at Skegness. President Mitterand of France drives the new *Train à Grande Vitesse* at 250kph.
Wednesday *September 23*	A statue of Winnie the Pooh is unveiled at London Zoo: the original bear lived there between 1914 and 1934! Autumn equinox
Thursday *September 24*	Steve Ovett loses wheelchair race at East Sussex Special Schools sports day in Brighton.
Friday *September 25*	Opening of £20,000 concrete bobsleigh run at Thorpe Park in Surrey: the sleighs have wheels instead of runners.
Saturday *September 26*	Wally the walrus flies home to the Arctic in a Boeing 727 from Heathrow.
Sunday *September 27*	*Sunday Times* Fun Run in Hyde Park: 27,000 people take part.

Monday *September 28*	Skyship 500, a huge helium filled airship makes a 2-hour flight, reaching 426m and speeds of 80kph, at Cardington, Bedfordshire. New Moon
Tuesday *September 29*	Jewish New Year. Wild mink invade waterways, lakes and ponds in the west country.
Wednesday *September 30*	US Government abandons project to listen for signals from other civilizations in the Milky Way with giant radio receivers.

STAMP OUT CIGARETTES.
You can 'LIVE' without them!

Never say yes to a Cigarette.

Wettest September in Glasgow for 100 years!

Driest summer on record in Gloucestershire. Only 80.6mm of rain in the past three months.

11km of river at the source of the Thames has dried up.

Pelicans!

Two pelicans were transferred from St James's Park in London to Regent's Park Zoo because they had been eating too many pigeons and duckling and not enough of their proper diet of whiting and mackerel. One of them, an EasternWhite, had been at the Park for more than 17 years, and the other, a Russian pelican called Kahn, had been there for nearly 4 years. There has ben a colony of pelicans in St James's Park since the time of King Charles II, who first imported them to England.

Wally the Walrus

Walruses live in the Arctic waters and are hardly ever seen around the coast of Great Britain: in fact, there have been only 20 sightings since 1830. Wally, who weighs half a tonne, was first seen off the Scottish coast at the beginning of September. He was then spotted on a beach in Lincolnshire before next turning up in the river Ouse—obviously very lost! Helicopters tried to rescue him but he headed back to sea before collapsing exhausted, on the beach at Skegness. It is almost impossible to keep walruses in captivity, so it was decided to fly him home to Greenland by plane. He travelled in a huge wooden crate.

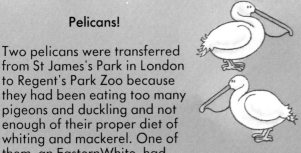

NO.1   9p
INDEPENDENCE FOR BELIZE, THE LAST BRITISH COLONY IN THE AMERICAS

DAILY CHATTER   10p
£40,000,000 IN GOLD SALVAGED FROM THE SUNK CRUISER H.M.S EDINBURGH

THE BEAVER   12p
BLACKPOOL ILLUMINATIONS SWITCHED ON. THE 375,000 LIGHT BULBS COST £770,000!

THE HOOT.   10p
EUROPEAN TUG-OF-WAR CHAMPIONSHIPS AT FOLKESTONE, KENT.

October

Thursday
October 1

The 654th Lord Mayor of London is elected at the Guildhall 12 noon.

Avalanche warnings in the Swiss Alps!

Friday
October 2

A senior government official in China dismisses reports in the press about children who can read with their ears as ridiculous.

Saturday
October 3

More than 140 people have died in Spain from the effects of a deadly cooking oil.

Sunday
October 4

Pearly Harvest Festival Service at St Martin's-in-the-Fields in Trafalgar Square, London.

Monday
October 5

A British educational satellite UOSAT (University of Surrey Satellite) goes into orbit.

Tuesday
October 6

20,000 eggs are smashed during a break-in at a packing station at Taunton, Somerset.

Wednesday
October 7

End of 'the most successful diving operation ever carried out'! Gold bars worth £43,000,000 have been recovered from *HMS Edinburgh*, 244m down in the Barents Sea.

Thursday
October 8

The lake in St James's Park, London is being drained and cleaned: it will probably take until next January!

Friday
October 9

Canterbury by-pass is opened. It cost £9,000,000 to build. Force 10 gales in the English Channel. Fallen trees block roads in the South, Suffolk and Essex. The Severn Bridge is closed to high-sided vehicles.

Tropical storm Lydia hits Mexico and kills 65 people

Saturday
October 10

Richard Noble becomes the fastest Briton on land in *Thrust Two* at 418.118mph (668.99 kph) across Bonneville Salt Flats in Utah, USA. He beats the record of 403.1mph (644.96 kph) set by Donald Campbell in *Bluebird* in 1964. [The world record is 622mph (995.2 kph).]

Sunday
October 11

World Conker Championships at Ashton, near Oundle, in Northamptonshire.

Monday
October 12

Square crisps have proved so popular that Smiths are buying more land for potato growing in Lincolnshire.

Full Moon

Tuesday
October 13

London Zoo announces that Ching Ching is not pregnant after all.

Happy Birthday Mrs Thatcher—56 today!

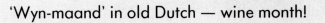

October

'Wyn-maand' in old Dutch — wine month!

From the Latin word 'octo' which means eight: it used to be the eighth month in the old Roman calendar.
'Winter-fylleth' in Old English, which means winter full moon.

1981 A Very Important Year for Conservation

In 1975 only two kinds of bats, the smooth snake, the sand lizard, the natterjack toad and the Large Blue butterfly were given full protection. In 1981 The Wildlife and Countryside Act which became law in October protected lots more species:

Adder	Grass Snake
Horseshoe Bats (all species)	Ladybird Spider
Rainbow Leaf Beetle	Common Toad
Heath Fritillary Butterfly	Burbot
Swallowtail Butterfly	Field Cricket
Bottle-nosed Dolphin	Sand Lizard
Norfolk Aeshna Dragonfly	Palmate Newt
Wart-biter Grasshopper	Harbour porpoise
Barbary Carpet Moth	Glutinous Snail
New Forest Burnet Moth	Smooth Snake
Great Crested Newt	Black-veined Moth
Common Otter	Typical Bats (all species)
Carthusian Snail	Chequered Skipper Butterfly
Large Blue Butterfly	Smooth Newt
Mole Cricket	Slow-worm
Common Dolphin	Sandbowl Snail
Common Frog	Fen Raft Spider
Viviparous Lizard	Red Squirrel
Essex Emerald Moth	Natterjack Toad
Reddish Buff Moth	

THE DAILY TRUNK 9p

CHILDREN CANNOT READ WITH THEIR EARS SAYS CHINESE GOVERNMENT

WEEKLY STAMP 10p

SIXTY SHEEP GET FALSE TEETH

YIPPEE 16p

MOUSE AUCTION AT ALEXANDRA PALACE

DAILY PUFF 10p

THE TREASURE OF H.M.S EDINBURGH

Wednesday *October 14*	American attempt to climb Everest fails at 7997.95m because of bad weather. Open Day at Hastings Castle to commemorate the battle on this day in 1066
Thursday *October 15*	The Greater London Council's transport department demonstrates the wheel clamp—already in use in France and the United States!
Friday *October 16*	Sixty sheep have been fitted with false teeth at the Ministry of Agriculture's farm in Herefordshire to make eating easier.
Saturday *October 17*	Mrs Elizabeth Forsdick, the first female official in the history of the FA Cup, is a 'linesperson' at a match between Burgess Hill and Carshalton Athletic.
Sunday *October 18*	*You Can do the Cube*, a 112-page book by Patrick Bossert (13), has sold more than 500,000 copies since August. It's also at the top of *The New York Times* best-seller list!
Monday *October 19*	3 tugs stranded on the rocks in St Bride's Bay, Dyfed.
Tuesday *October 20*	A large hole (3m x 2m) has appeared in the left paw of the 4500-year-old Great Sphinx of Giza in Egypt.
Wednesday *October 21*	The annual Honey Show at Caxton Hall in London. Scientists warn of a global warming because of the burning of fossil fuels: could lead to the ice caps melting.
Thursday *October 22*	The average man in Britain is 1.78m tall and weighs 73.48kg.
Friday *October 23*	Staff at the Natural History Museum celebrate its centenary in the Central Hall with a cake in the shape of the museum.
Saturday *October 24*	Traffic in central London is brought to a halt by a national CND demonstration: tens of thousands march from the Embankment to Hyde Park Corner.
Sunday *October 25*	The New York Marathon: out of 16,000 entrants, Alberto Salazar wins in the world's best time of 2 hrs 8 mins 13 secs. Allison Roe beats the women's best time with 2 hrs 25 mins 29 secs.
Monday *October 26*	British Telecom introduce 'tele-messages' to replace the telegram: £3 for up to 50 words and names, addresses and even post codes go free!

New Moon

Tuesday *October 27*	A 60m Whiskey-class Soviet submarine, with 55 crew on board runs aground only 16km from a Swedish naval base.
Wednesday *October 28*	The Prince and Princess of Wales attend an 800th anniversary service at St David's Cathedral in Wales in torrential rain. The Princess says her first word of Welsh *'Diolch'*, which means 'thank you'!
Thursday *October 29*	Paul Rodgers, Britain's solo yachtsman, who is trying to circumnavigate the world twice, sets off again from Fremantle, Australia, where he put in with a broken mast and cracked ribs.
Friday *October 30*	The Soviet Union launch an unmanned space-craft *Venera 13*, which is expected to reach Venus next March.
Saturday *October 31*	Hallowe'en! Mouse auction at the London Championship show at the Alexandra Palace in London.

'DIOLCH'

Sports Highlights

Ian Botham held more catches (except for the wicket-keeper), took more wickets, and scored more runs than any other English player in the history of Test cricket.

Sebastian Coe broke the mile record twice in the greatest ten days of middle distance running that the world has ever seen. He took it in Zurich in 3 minutes 48.53 seconds, only to be robbed of it by Steve Ovett in Koblenz in 3 minutes 48.4 seconds. Coe then went on to win it back in Brussels in 3 minutes 47.33 seconds.

Jayne Torvill and Christopher Dean won the European title for ice dancing in February, and then the world title in March, when five of the judges gave them 5.9 out of 6 for artistic impression.

Bob Champion had two major operations for cancer in 1979, recovered fully, and went on to win the Grand National on *Aldaniti*, a chestnut gelding who had only raced once before this season.

November

Sunday
November 1

London to Brighton Veteran Car Run: it commemorates Emancipation Day in 1896, when the law requiring motor vehicles to have someone walking in front with a red flag was abolished!

Monday
November 2

Citizens Band radio becomes legal.

All schools in Saudi Arabia closed today so that pupils and teachers can pray for rain.

Tuesday
November 3

Twenty-fifth London Film Festival. Plans for a new film museum are announced (MOMI).

Wednesday
November 4

US space shuttle *Columbia*'s second launch is postponed 31 secs before take-off.

Thursday
November 5

A Royal Announcement: the Princess of Wales is expecting a baby!

NEW ROYAL BABY

Friday
November 6

The Queen opens the new £280,000,000 Metro system in Newcastle.

Saturday
November 7

£1,000's worth of lizards, frogs and 1 terrapin are stolen from the reptile house at London Zoo this week-end.

Sunday
November 8

Remembrance Sunday. Uproar in the popular press about the duffle coat Michael Foot, the leader of the Labour Party, wears at the Cenotaph service in Whitehall.

Monday
November 9

The Royal Mint is striking a £5 gold proof coin. It's the first time one has been issued during the reign of Queen Elizabeth II.

£5·00

Tuesday
November 10

Sammy the Snail, who spent 3 years as an ornament on a dressing table, wakes up and is released at Gibraltar Point near Skegness.

Full Moon

Wednesday
November 11

A lifeboat coxswain, an RAF rescue helicopter pilot, a policeman, a champion sprinter and a top snooker player are among the chief guests at the Men of the Year lunch.

Thursday
November 12

Columbia becomes the first space-craft in the world to be launched twice — with 85 dwarf sunflowers on board.

Friday
November 13

The first helium-filled balloon to cross the Pacific—which travelled nearly 9656km in $3\frac{1}{2}$ days—crash lands in California. It's the longest non-stop balloon ride ever made!

Saturday
November 14

Lord Mayor's Show in London, with a fireworks display from barges moored on the river Thames by Blackfriars Bridge.

November

Takes its name from the Latin word for nine 'novem', because it used to be the ninth month in the old Roman calendar, when the year began in March.

The old Saxon name was 'Wind-monath'—wind month!

The old Dutch name was 'Slaght-maand'—slaughter month.

Flowers and Plants Protected by the Wildlife and Countryside Act 1981

In 1975, 21 wild flowers were protected from picking and uprooting. In 1981 the list was extended to 60 species.

Small Alison
Bedstraw Broomrape
Oxtongue Broomrape
Thistle Broomrape
Alpine Catchfly
Rock Cinquefoil
Triangular Club-rush
Wild Cotoneaster
Field Cow-wheat
Jersey Cudweed
Diapensia
Field Eryngo
Dickie's Bladder Fern
Killarney Fern
Brown Galingale
Alpine Gentian
Spring Gentian
Water Germander
Wild Gladiolus
Sickle-leaved Hare's-ear
Small Hare's-ear

Blue Heath
Red Helleborine
Perennial Knawel
Sea Knotgrass
Lady's-slipper
Sea Lavender
Least Lettuce
Round-headed Leek
Rough Marsh-mallow
Early Spider Orchid
Fen Orchid
Ghost Orchid
Late Spider Orchid
Lizard Orchid
Military Orchid
Monkey Orchid
Plymouth Pear
Cheddar Pink
Childling Pink
Norwegian Sandwort
Teesdale Sandwort

Drooping Saxifrage
Tufted Saxifrage
Whorled
    Solomon's-seal
Alpine Sow-thistle
Adder's-tongue
    Spearwort
Spiked Speedwell
Purple Spurge
Starfruit
Fen Violet
Ribbon leaved
    Water-plantain
Starved Wood-sedge
Alpine Woodsia
Oblong Woodsia
Field Wormwood
Downy Woundwort
Limestone Woundwort
Greater Yellow-rattle
Snowdon Lily

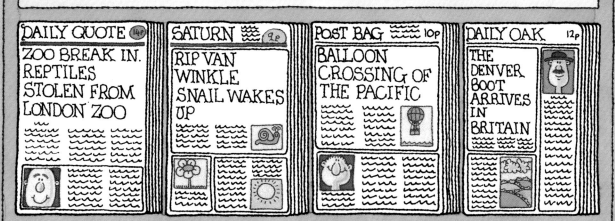

DAILY QUOTE 14p
ZOO BREAK IN. REPTILES STOLEN FROM LONDON ZOO

SATURN 9p
RIP VAN WINKLE SNAIL WAKES UP

POST BAG 10p
BALLOON CROSSING OF THE PACIFIC

DAILY OAK 12p
THE DENVER BOOT ARRIVES IN BRITAIN

Sunday *November 15*	Six Red Devils parachute 914.4m into Hampshire to bring the first Beaujolais Nouveau from France at 12.22am!
Monday *November 16*	The fifteenth-century Great Tower at Magdalen College, Oxford is restored after 6 years. It cost £900,000.
Tuesday *November 17*	The bugler plays the Last Post for Charlie the ship's cat, who is buried with full naval honours at Chatham Naval Base.
Wednesday *November 18*	The Post Office issues special children's Christmas stamps: Samantha Brown (5) designed the 11½ pence one.
Thursday *November 19*	The Prince and Princess of Wales plant 6 cherry trees in Hyde Park.
Friday *November 20*	World chess champion, Anatoly Karpov, beats Viktor Korchnoi 6—2 to keep his world title.
Saturday *November 21*	Miniature deer called Muntjacks, which escaped from Woburn Abbey park during the last war, are spotted in Sherwood Forest!
Sunday *November 22*	The Central Line, between Leyton and Bethnal Green in London, is stopped while two 14-storey tower blocks are demolished.
Monday *November 23*	Australia — United States Boomerang Test in Sydney. Parking metre charges in central London are doubled to 60p an hour.
Tuesday *November 24*	You can go inside the stone circle at Stonehenge again for the first time since 1978, but only on winter Tuesdays!
Wednesday *November 25*	A litter of piglets named after the Seven Dwarfs make their first appearance at London Zoo. They will only grow 30 cm tall!
Thursday *November 26*	Princess Margaret goes to lunch at the Savoy Hotel in London to present the awards to the Champion Children of the Year. New Moon
Friday *November 27*	Jasper, the yellow labrador, injured by a booby-trap bomb outside Woolwich Barracks, goes home after his front left leg was saved.
Saturday *November 28*	For sale, in Dallas, Texas: a 1.37m robot who can dust, clean, serve refreshments and take the dog for a walk. Price: £7,500.
Sunday *November 29*	The RSPB has bought 1618 hectares of the Island of Yell in the Shetlands. The population includes curlew, lapwing, otters and seals.
Monday *November 30*	Harold Welling retires as manager of the Lost Property Office: during his time 2,000,000 umbrellas, were found!

'IN' IN 1981

Roller skates
Pop-up books
Jellybeans
Strawberry Shortcake dolls (that smelled of strawberries)
Sleepings bags that looked like bananas, cucumbers, corn-on-the-cob or
chocolate eclairs
Woks
Walkmans
Lady Di
Knickerbockers

'OUT' IN 1981

Lord Lucan, who disappeared seven years ago, is declared officially dead.
Airfix Industries, the Dinky Toys and Meccano Group, collapsed, owing £15,000,000.
NOW! weekly news magazine
Lights on the Eddystone Lighthouse are put out for a year while it goes automatic.
HRH Princess Alice of Athlone, Jack Warner who played Dixon of Dock Green, Bob Marley who brought reggae to UK, Moshe Dyan, Mike Hailwood (ten times world motor cycle racing champion) all die.

WHAT DIDN'T HAPPEN IN 1981

After months of waiting, Ching Ching wasn't pregnant, after all! Neither was Ling Ling at Washington Zoo—even though Chia Chia made a special Transatlantic trip from London Zoo.

WHAT CAME AND WENT IN 1981

The Advanced Passenger Train, which made a record-breaking journey from Glasgow to London, but had too much trouble with its tilt.

WHAT DIDN'T CATCH ON IN 1981

Perfumed tennis balls
Yellow telephone boxes

December

Tuesday
December 1

The Dutch yacht *Flyer* is leading in the Round the World Yacht Race off the north east coast of New Zealand.

Wednesday
December 2

TV licenses go up from £34 to £46 for colour and from £12 to £15 for black-and-white sets.

Thursday
December 3

Grand Prix of the International Exhibition of Inventions at Geneva goes to John Cruse, from Robertsbridge, Sussex, for a new automatic way of sowing perfectly-spaced seeds.

Friday
December 4

A record is set by two Bewick Swans who have returned for the ninth year in a row from Russia to the Welney Bird Reserve near Wisbech in Cambridgeshire. Altogether, they've now brought 35 cygnets to the reserve.

Saturday
December 5

For sale at Harrods: Californian hermit crabs. £1.50 for the 2.5cm size, £2.50 for the 7.6cm ones.

Sunday
December 6

'Little Ben', the 9m high distant relative of 'Big Ben', is put back at the junction of Victoria Street and Vauxhall Bridge Road, London, after 17 years.

Monday
December 7

British Rail's Advanced Passenger Train makes its record breaking maiden run from Glasgow to London in 4 hrs 13 mins 59 secs.

Tuesday
December 8

You can telephone Father Christmas from today on 246 8020 (London), 8020—preceded by the area code (outside London).

Wednesday
December 9

The BIG FREEZE continues! –13°C Dumfries (only – 11°C in Iceland). Father Christmas has a party for 60 children at 11 Downing Street in London.

Thursday
December 10

The last broadside ever from the Royal Navy: the destroyer *London* fires its four 4.5ins guns, 24km off Plymouth, on its last trip home from a Caribbean tour.

Full Moon

Friday
December 11

'Big Ben' freezes to a halt between 12.27 and 1.30pm.
Mrs Thatcher throws snowballs at cameramen in Shropshire.

Worst blizzards for thirty years! –27°C at Carnwath in Strathclyde: 3-1 on for a white Christmas

Saturday
December 12

The British Rubik Cube Championship in London: the winner is Julian Chivers (15) from Norwich, with a world record time of 25.75secs!

Sunday *December 13*	Ideal Christmas presents: solid gold sunglasses £1100, solid gold beard rake £825, and champagne-flavoured tooth-paste, £1.99!

Sub-zero temperatures everywhere:
The coldest December in Britain since 1895

Monday *December 14*	The first of the 4 huge main gates for the Thames Barrier, between Silvertown and Charlton, is moved into place.
Tuesday *December 15*	The Home Office launches a new film for children 'Say No To Strangers'.
Wednesday *December 16*	Ten children receive awards as Children of Courage 1981.
Thursday *December 17*	Last day for posting second-class Christmas cards in the UK. The government rejects call to phase out the battery cage system of producing eggs.

December

Takes its name from the Latin word for ten 'decem' — it used to be the tenth month in the old Roman calendar.

CHILDREN OF COURAGE 1981
Mark King (4 years), from Lincoln
Anthony Hynes (4 years), from Huddersfield
Charlotte Duffy (5 years), from Aylesbury
Darren Daly (9 years), from Surrey
Ashley Bailey (9 years), from Upholland, Lancashire
Donna McGuire (10 years), from Plymouth
Sarah Tuck (9 years), from Chippenham, Wiltshire
Sonia Segovia (11 years) from White City, London
Anne Marie Jamieson (7 years), from Kilbirnie, Ayrshire
Michelle Pocock (10 years), from Eastbourne

LAST MINUTE CHRISTMAS PRESENTS

A glass dome containing a million dollars — shredded, £55

A Fossilized dinosaur's egg, £750

WHITE CHRISTMAS CHART
1906, 1927, 1938 and 1970 with the odd snowflake in 1962 and 1968!

Friday *December 18*	The final countdown for the last test flight of the European rocket *Ariane* gets under way: scheduled lift-off 1.30pm GMT December 20.
Saturday *December 19*	Last day for posting first-class Christmas cards in the UK. Roads into Imber, the 'lost village' on the Salisbury Plain, which was taken over by the Army in the last war, are open to the public until January 3.
Sunday *December 20*	The Penlee lifeboat from Mousehole, Cornwall, with an 8-man crew, sinks in heavy seas trying to rescue the coaster *Union Star*.
Monday *December 21*	The noise level of ice-cream vans is to be restricted to 4sec bursts. The Electric Palace Cinema, Harwich, which closed in 1956, opens for a short Christmas run of Walt Disney films.
Tuesday *December 22*	Dial-a-Carol starts today! Chia Chia is out of 6 months quarantine after his trip to the USA. He is re-united with Ching Ching.
Wednesday *December 23*	Geoff Boycott scores 86 not out, in the Third Test against India in Delhi—beating Sir Gary Sobers' record of 8032 runs in Test cricket! More Snow
Thursday *December 24*	Middleweight turkeys (between 6 and 7kg) are the most popular this year. They cost 75—90p per 500gms (fresh).
Friday *December 25*	No snow falls on the roof of the Meteorological Office in London so it's not an Official White Christmas after all! New Moon
Saturday *December 26*	Watch out for the sawbill duck family now—winter visitors with toothed beaks, who dive for fish. There are three kinds: goosanders, red-breasted mergansers and smew.
Sunday *December 27*	The Queen's Christmas Message is translated into sign language for the first time.
Monday *December 28*	Three women and 2 dogs set up a peace camp near RAF Molesworth in Cambridgeshire, where US Cruise missiles are going to be based in 1983.
Tuesday *December 29*	Thirty police and RSPCA men abandon bear hunt on Hackney marshes, started when prints were spotted in the snow.
Wednesday *December 30*	The big THAW! High winds and heavy rain cause heavy flooding.
Thursday *December 31*	Sebastian Coe and Steve Ovett become MBEs in the New Year's Honours List.